# In the Secret Place

# In the Secret Place

LIFECHANGE BOOKS

# J. OTIS
# LEDBETTER

Multnomah® Publishers *Sisters, Oregon*

IN THE SECRET PLACE
published by Multnomah Publishers, Inc.

© 2003 by J. Otis Ledbetter
International Standard Book Number: 1-59052-252-4

Cover design by Steve Gardner
Cover image by Veer, Inc.

Unless otherwise indicated, Scripture quotations are from:
*The Holy Bible,* New King James Version © 1984 by Thomas Nelson, Inc.
Other Scripture quotations are from:
*The Holy Bible,* New International Version (NIV) © 1973, 1984 by
International Bible Society, used by permission of Zondervan Publishing House
The Randy Alcorn quotation in chapter five
is from his article "Can Demons Read Our Thoughts?"
on the Eternal Perspective Ministries website: www.epm.org.

*Multnomah* is a trademark of Multnomah Publishers, Inc.,
and is registered in the U.S. Patent and Trademark Office.
The colophon is a trademark of Multnomah Publishers, Inc.

For information:
MULTNOMAH PUBLISHERS, INC. • P.O. BOX 1720 • SISTERS, OR 97759
Library of Congress Cataloging-in-Publication Data

Ledbetter, J. Otis.
  In the secret place : for God and you alone / by J. Otis Ledbetter.
      p. cm.
  ISBN 1-59052-252-4
  1. Christian life—Biblical teaching. 2. Prayer—Biblical teaching. I. Title.
BS680.C47L43 2003
248.4—dc21
                              2003008851
          03 04 05 06 07 08—10 9 8 7 6 5 4 3 2 1 0

*To my wife Gail,*
*who was given to me by the One*
*from whom all good and perfect gifts come!*

# Contents

# ACKNOWLEDGMENTS

To my friends Steve VanWinkle and Kurt Bruner whose passion for words helped shape the embryonic message of this book, and to Jim Weidmann for taking the step to expose its contents to the publisher. My deepest gratitude to Doug Gabbert and Thomas Womack who saw the need to get this message into a purposeful manuscript. And to my strong right arm and constant friend Sherry Krigbaum for her protecting encouragement.

# Chapter One

# THE PLACE WE'VE ALWAYS WANTED

*In You I take shelter.*
*Teach me to do Your will,*
*for You are my God.*
PSALM 143:9–10

In the church where my father was a pastor during my boyhood, a set of stairs behind the sanctuary led upward to some classrooms. Tucked away beneath those steps was an abandoned janitor's closet with only one entrance—a narrow doorway just big enough for my slim body to slip through.

That's where I would go when I wanted to be alone just to think. That's where I could occupy my mind with the typical struggles of a nine- or ten-year-old—my budding, innocent romances, my schoolyard sports career.

Then came the day when one of my friends in the church died of a childhood disease. Suddenly my secret place took on a whole new significance. I spent a lot of time there, pondering my own mortality. The issue consumed me, and what I remember most is how fearful I was. That little closet was the only space where I could think through such a terrifying matter and come away feeling better about it.

Meanwhile my father's church was growing, which eventually prompted our relocation to a new church facility that didn't provide me with the hideaway I'd grown accustomed to. I grew into my teen years still wanting such a place, but never quite finding one—a suitable location where I could escape the disturbing everydayness and confusing choices of adolescence, a place where I could enter and no one else could, a place of solitude where I could hear the clear leading of the Lord.

## A Place More Real

As manhood dawned on me, I began to wonder if what I was seeking wasn't a physical location, but something else, something deeper and more real.

As my "life verse" I had earlier claimed the entire ninety-first Psalm, which begins, "He who dwells in the secret place of the Most High shall abide under the shadow of the Almighty." As time went by, the fuller meaning of those words began to grip me more and more. Little by little I came to see there really was a secret place where God wanted me to meet with Him—not a closet or room, but a real place nevertheless, a place of fellowship where I could go anytime and pour out the questions and hurts of my heart in the presence of my Father. It was where I could hear directly from God about my life's decisions, and He would always be there to give me all the time and answers I needed to face the turmoils and traumas of my life.

*I came to see there really was a secret place where God wanted me to meet with Him.*

Even without fully understanding this truth, I began to use it.

A close friend and I had decided to pursue careers as certified public accountants, and we decided together on the college we wanted to attend to get started on this pursuit. But even while we were pushing forward our plans, in my newly found secret place I sensed a moving in my spirit; deep in my heart I came to realize that those plans would never happen. God was preparing something different for me, though it took a while for me to discover what this direction would be.

## UNIQUELY DESIGNED

So it was that I learned early to withdraw often to this place and commune with God. Experiencing the Lord's presence in the secret place has been a source of refreshment throughout my Christian life; there, my God and I have planned His business for me.

I believe from God's Word that He has provided such a secret place for each of His children to dwell with Him, a place He uniquely designed for each one in order to communicate His will to them. It isn't something only for the spiritual *haves,* to the exclusion of the *have-nots* (a demeaning distinction I don't believe in). God has a secret place waiting for you and for every believer—and the choice whether to meet Him there is entirely our own.

*When He created you, He knew you would need a private place to meet Him.*

No one knows your needs better than your Father in heaven. When He created you, He knew you would need a private place to meet Him—a place where no one else may enter, a pathway where only you and He can stroll. He calls it "the secret place" (not just "a" secret place) because there's only one like it for each of us. And we need look no further than the Scriptures to determine its location.

Tragically, however, intimacy with God in the secret place—one of the most powerful spiritual realities our Lord has given us—remains unknown to many of the very people He intends to be blessed by it. In fact, some of them still doubt this place's existence even after being told of it. But we must not allow the tactics of the evil one to take this blessing away from us through his deceptive power to convince us there's no such place.

## CONNECTION AND PROTECTION

As a pastor, I can't begin to number the times people have wished aloud in counseling sessions that they somehow had a clearer connection with God and His guidance. As one man expressed it, "I just wish God would write down His instructions for me and send it in a letter."

Others feel discouraged because of a seeming inability to escape ever-present pressures from the evil one. For them, "doing business" with God always seems ineffective; "I just can never seem to get away from Satan's influence," they say. They conclude that the devil must be able to read their every thought, and constant spiritual defeat overshadows their life as a result. As they're frustrated once more by an event or circumstance that in hindsight seems to be yet another example of the enemy's snares, they wonder: "Why couldn't God have warned me about that without Satan interfering?"

When I explain to these beleaguered people about the secret place—about their own private stronghold in the presence of their God, a place where they can discern His personal and unique directions for their life through the promptings of His Spirit, a place that's entirely off-limits to intrusion by Satan and the demonic forces under his dominion—a look of relief crosses their face.

May that same sense of relief be yours throughout this book as we discover more about encountering God in the secret place.

# Chapter Two

# RESERVED
# FOR TWO

*My soul thirsts for God, for the living God.*
*When shall I come and appear before God?*
PSALM 42:2

As you weigh the significance of this concept I'm describing, you may wonder: Is the secret place nothing more than getting away to think on your own? There doesn't seem to be anything special about that—even an unbeliever can get alone with his thoughts.

And that's exactly it! "Alone with his thoughts" is the situation for the unbeliever; God's children, however, come to the secret place to be with their Father. The secret place of the believer always has a reservation for two.

## WHERE IS IT?

So what is the secret place? And where is it?

Though it's a real place, it transcends any spatial dimensions. And it's invisible. It isn't something we ascertain by any of our five senses. Even if someone could somehow throw a switch to turn off your eyesight, your hearing, and your senses of smell and taste and touch, you could still encounter God in the secret place. He created our five senses so we might enjoy the beauty of His creation and operate effectively within its reality, but He can bypass those senses and work directly within our spirits to communicate His certain presence and everything He wants us to know.

*Though it's a real place, it transcends spatial dimensions.*

Jesus often said, "He who has ears to hear, let him hear." I believe He was speaking of more than physical ears and physical hearing, and of more than just the specific words He uttered on those occasions to the particular people gathered around Him at the time. He was speaking also of His audible voice to His followers down through the centuries, and of their ability to distinguish and understand it through the Holy Spirit's enablement within them.

The secret place isn't some mystical or magical location where God plays hide-and-seek with us. It is, however, a spiritual place, far below your skin and muscle and sinew, deeper than your vital organs, with more life-sustaining value than your blood vessels and giving you more strength than your bone structure. It's a place lying in the depths of your spirit, so deep that no one else but you and God can get there. The map showing the way is legible to no one else. No other person, no matter how powerful, and no matter how cherished he or she may be to you, can visit its confines—not even your spouse, your children, your closest friend. You may be able to describe this place to them, but they cannot make an entrance there to experience it simultaneously with you.

## WHEN DO WE GO THERE?

The kind of devotional time that many believers set aside each day is only a glimpse of what God offers in the secret place. He often calls us there at other times to communicate with us.

His invitations to join Him there often seem to come in the middle of the night or in the dark hours before dawn. We sense His wakening call in much the same way the boy Samuel did in 1 Samuel 3. Anytime I'm awakened for no apparent reason during the night, I always think first, *God, are You wanting to talk to me in the secret place?* Sometimes I turn over and fall asleep again, but most times I sense a strong prompting to meet with Him.

This has particularly been true during the past five

years, as the church and the private Christian school I lead have been building and growing. As decision points and financial deadlines approached, God has often awakened me to meet with Him, and in the secret place He has settled my heart and confirmed His control over the details.

I'm often amused as to why this needs to happen at such weird hours. Perhaps I'm not as diligent in committing such matters into His hands during normal hours. Or maybe He just wants my undivided attention, and that's the perfect opportunity to get it. You may find Him frequently doing the same thing with You, especially as you move into greater intimacy with God in the secret place.

## What Happens There?

Although in the Scripture we sometimes see God sending visions and angels to communicate His will to individuals, for believers today the word *promptings* probably best describes how God's Spirit communicates with us in the secret place.

Those promptings from the Lord are as real today as ever. Not long ago, my wife Gail and I set aside an evening to drop by some homes of the new people who had been visiting our church. Our intent was to make a brief appearance, letting the family know how much we enjoyed their visits to our Sunday services. We were frustrated in our efforts. No one answered their doors, so we headed home.

Not far from the turnoff to our house, Gail said to me, "Keith and Dianne have been on my heart all day." These were friends of ours and former neighbors, but after moving from their neighborhood we'd lost touch with them. "The Lord must be prompting me to pray for Dianne," Gail said. "Why don't we stop by and see if they're home?"

I turned the car around and headed for their house.

We walked up the drive to their front door and rang the bell. Keith answered the door. His jaw dropped and he uttered some unintelligible sound, then invited us in.

*'I asked God to send someone by...and here you are!'*

As we were sitting down, he explained his amazement. "Just twenty minutes ago I knelt beside my couch and prayed. Today has been almost unbearable. So tonight I asked God to send someone by to pray with me...and here you are!"

After prayer together and some uplifting fellowship with our friends, Gail and I left overwhelmed once again with how God guides us by means of the secret place.

## GOD'S WORD COMES ALIVE

The secret place provides the right environment where we're most free to sense the genuine promptings of God's

Spirit. But a word of caution is in order, lest you think that in the secret place God reveals things that go against or beyond the truths in Holy Scripture.

In the freedom from the world's distractions that we find in the secret place, God shines His light on His written Word in our hearts and makes plain how it applies to our personal circumstances.

Such personal understanding of the Bible is especially essential in weighing desires or plans we have. In the light of Scripture, we can determine if these are rising from our own selfish desires or confirm that they're actually a prompting from God.

Those are some perspectives relating to basic questions about the secret place. But to understand it best, let's look in the pages of Scripture to the passages that speak most directly about this freeing and wonderful truth. Get ready for a rich time in exploring God's Word.

*Chapter Three*

# OUT OF THE CHAOS, INTO THE CALM

*For those who trust in You…*
*You shall hide them in the secret place of Your presence.*
PSALM 31:19–20

Especially when danger swirled around him, David—the man after God's own heart—learned to cherish his own secret place in the Lord's presence. Look at how he sings about it in the twenty-seventh Psalm:

> For in the time of trouble
>     He shall hide me in His pavilion;
> *In the secret place* of His tabernacle
>     He shall hide me.

V. 5

In the secret place, David becomes totally aware of being completely protected—and that same experience can also be yours.

In the secret place you can find full assurance of personal victory in the Lord, just as David does: "He shall set me high upon a rock. And now my head shall be lifted up above my enemies all around me" (vv. 5–6).

Are you facing any threat or hardship at this time that makes you anxious or fearful? In the secret place you can recover the same fresh awareness of God and the same ability to cast off fear that David sings about in this psalm. Just listen to his God-given confidence:

> The LORD is my light and my salvation;
> Whom shall I fear?
> The LORD is the strength of my life;
> Of whom shall I be afraid?…
> Though an army may encamp against me,
> My heart shall not fear;
> Though war should rise against me,
> In this I will be confident.
>
> VV. I, 3

## THE ONE THING WE DESIRE

For David—and for you and me—the secret place is more than a place of protection and confidence-building. It's the environment for resting in the very dwelling place of God, the very presence of God.

David describes his secret place as an entry into God's "pavilion" and "tabernacle" (Psalm 27:5); it ushers him into "the house of the Lord" and "His temple" (v. 4). In David's lifetime, the glorious and beautiful temple that would rise on Mount Zion in Jerusalem had not yet been constructed; David's eyes at this moment are on a place even more glorious and beautiful, the temple in heaven where he communes with God by way of the secret place. Your eyes can look there too.

*David concludes that being with God in the secret place is the ultimate experience.*

Your own secret place is where you, like David, can "behold the beauty of the LORD" (v. 4)—enjoying your unique individual experience of God as He reveals Himself to you with an intimacy that brings more inner satisfaction than anything else possibly could. In such intimacy you can "inquire in His temple," just as David does (v. 4), laying before Him your every need, your every concern, your every question, and finding God's help and answers.

No wonder David joyfully concludes that being with God in the secret place is the "one thing" he desires of the Lord, the ultimate experience he seeks (v. 4). This will be your lasting desire as well as you continue to meet with God in the secret place.

## PRESCRIPTION FOR PEACE

In the Bible, my favorite look inside the secret place comes in Psalm 91, a passage I strongly urge you to turn to as soon as possible as you explore and get acquainted with your secret place. Allow God to personalize the message of this psalm for you, engraving it into your soul as a vision and a guarantee of the blessedness He has in store for you there.

*How much of life is influenced by potentially negative forces outside our control?*

The unnamed author of this psalm gives us a guided tour of a restful, safe place that's like a veritable oasis for the longing or fearful spirit. In this place, chaos is absent, calmness is in abundance. It's a prescription for peace from the Great Physician.

Rest...safety...calmness...peace.... For most of us, those words don't exactly describe life as usual. Why is that?

Have you ever thought about how much of our lives is influenced by potentially negative forces outside our control? Listen to how the worst of such harmful uncertainties are vividly depicted in Psalm 91:

The snare...

The terror by night…
The arrow that flies by day…
The pestilence that walks in darkness…
The destruction that lays waste at noonday. (vv. 3–6)

Chilling terms—yet fully on the mark in describing how we can sometimes feel about the unexpected battles and challenges that flare up against us in life and corner our attention.

## TRAPPED BY THE UNCONTROLLABLE

When you think about it, isn't our anxiety over such uncontrollable factors and circumstances the very thing that often keeps us from accomplishing great things for God? Doesn't it hinder us from realizing our potential in Christ and pull us back from giving our best effort in whatever He calls us to?

We get trapped: "Like birds caught in a snare, so the sons of men are snared in an evil time, when it falls suddenly upon them" (Ecclesiastes 9:12).

Psalm 91 goes on to give another frightful image you may identify with: "A thousand may fall at your side, and ten thousand at your right hand" (v. 7). Have you noticed how the failures of others around you—spiritual failures, moral failures, relational failures, career failures, ministry failures—can dampen and wither your own motivation for success and accomplishment and your sense of security about the future? So many lives around us are littered with

*So many lives around us are littered with disappointments and breakdowns.*

disappointments and breakdowns, causing us to shy away ourselves from indulging in big dreams, from reaching for the stars and risking any part of life to accomplish big things. Our personal goals that once shone so brightly now seem too lofty and unrealistic.

## THE SHADOW THAT PROTECTS

So many discouraging obstacles in life, so many potential adversities! But you're responding properly to them when you let those fears and concerns drive you to the secret place, to reinforce its deepest lesson:

> He who dwells in the secret place of the Most High
> Shall abide under the shadow of the Almighty.
>
> v. 1

The secret place is where you deepen your capacity to abide calmly in Christ, to live constantly within His shadow.

By dwelling in the secret place, your faith in God will be energized. From the depths of your being, you'll sing along with the author of this psalm, "He is my refuge and my fortress; my God, in Him I will trust" (v. 2).

And what about those uncontrollable adversities, all that danger by day and danger by night? "Surely He shall deliver you…. You shall not be afraid" (vv. 3, 5).

Resting in the secret place, you'll find the bold conviction and confidence to hold on to the following words as your personal promise from God:

> No evil shall befall you,
> Nor shall any plague come near your dwelling.
>
> v. 10

And what about all the failure that strikes down so many others all around you? "It shall not come near you" (v. 7)!

With the eyes of your heart, this is how you'll see yourself in the enfolding protection of your loving God:

> He shall cover you with His feathers,
> And under His wings you shall take refuge;
> His truth shall be your shield and buckler.
>
> v. 4

Through the time you spend in the secret place, you'll also come to believe firmly in the reality and presence of God's guardian angels and their power in your own life and experience:

> For He shall give His angels charge over you,
> To keep you in all your ways.
> In their hands they shall bear you up,
> Lest you dash your foot against a stone.
>
> vv. 11–12

## Glimpsing Your Future

What's more, in the secret place your God-nurtured plans and His calling for your future will spring to life in your spiritual vision, and you'll be assured of vanquishing spiritual foes as you move forward in God's kingdom work and in spiritual warfare:

> You shall tread upon the lion and the cobra,
> The young lion and the serpent you shall trample
> underfoot.
>
> v. 13

Abiding in the secret place, you'll hear the words of Jesus as never before: "Behold, I give you the authority to trample on serpents and scorpions, and over all the power of the enemy, and nothing shall by any means hurt you" (Luke 10:19). The secret place is where your innermost spirit will get reconnected to the truth that if God is for you, no one can be against you (Romans 8:31).

These are the soaring promises and solid provisions for the man or woman who will abide with God in the secret place.

So go to the secret place, and let your loving Father personally deliver those promises to your heart!

# Chapter Four

# WHEN IT'S TIME
# FOR A CHANGE

*You will show me the path of life.*
PSALM 16:11

What would it take for God to move your life in a different direction—to make a major change in location or work or ministry? If you found yourself pondering such a change, how could you be certain God was behind it? And even if you were convinced the idea came from God, how could you be confident that you were developing and nurturing your plans for it in the wisest and safest way?

Facing those very issues allowed my wife and me to learn more about the strategic value of the secret place.

## A Choice to Make

In 1971, Gail and I moved to California after I was asked to become the worship leader in a church in the Los Angeles area. Not long after we arrived, I was offered a professorship at a nearby Christian college.

Over the next several years, Gail and I invested ourselves in establishing our family, a wide network of close friends, and thriving, fruit-bearing ministries at both the church and the college. We purchased our first house in a beautiful neighborhood and made it into a home that fit us perfectly.

We felt loved and appreciated, we were well taken care of financially, and our intention was to continuing serving the Lord together in these circumstances until retirement. Our kids were settled into their schools and had made fast friends. Gail was having success in her own ministry as a teacher. We had influence and we had opportunity to help shape lives and ministries for the future.

Meanwhile, my father had also come to California to pastor a church in Fresno, 250 miles north. I often visited the church over the years, and on several occasions I had been the guest speaker there.

When Dad reached his mid-seventies, he underwent quadruple bypass heart surgery, and the pressures of the pastorate were finally beginning to be too much for him. One Sunday afternoon I received a phone call from him. By the tone in his voice, I immediately sensed something was up. He quickly got to the point—and his news stunned me.

"The church here took a vote today," he said, "and they called you as pastor."

This came completely out of the blue, and I was too shocked to respond.

Filling the silence, Dad went on: "The vote was 100 percent."

I finally managed to speak. "Well, Dad, I'm not a candidate." With as much conviction as I could muster, I continued, "And furthermore, I'm happy where I am."

"Well then, I guess you have a choice to make," Dad said, with the sort of chuckle that told me he'd enjoyed blindsiding me.

*He quickly got to the point—and his news stunned me.*

Dad had always wanted one of his sons to work beside him, and I wondered if this was just another way of his expressing that desire. Or was God really calling my family to a new ministry? I'd never been a senior pastor, but when a church of a few hundred people votes unanimously to call someone, it isn't something to be ignored.

## NEEDING CRYSTAL-CLEAR GUIDANCE

I kept Dad's news to myself and pondered it repeatedly. My wife and I had often visited Fresno, though we actually knew little about the community or the area. And frankly, what we did know we didn't much like; we'd actually thanked God for not putting us in a place like that. Moreover, in my family's life, the time just didn't seem right to consider moving anywhere.

Yet God was working in my spirit, nudging me in the direction of Dad's church. I tried not to let my rising uncertainty show—and I was totally afraid to talk to Gail about how God was stirring me in the deepest part of my heart.

*God was working in my spirit, nudging me.*

No one but God and I knew of that stirring, so in the secret place I began to work out the details I needed for a confident decision. "God," I prayed silently and repeatedly, "if you can change my heart on this, then you can change Gail's also."

Although my dad and the people in his church knew the offer was on the table, I never spoke of it aloud to anyone around me. In fact, I never told Dad or anyone that I was having a change of heart. I knew that if any of Satan's forces discovered the direction my thoughts were moving, they might create distractions to muddy the clarity I needed to discern God's will. The enemy can do such things—both subtly and blatantly.

After weeks of doing spiritual business on this matter together with God, one morning I was sitting at my desk when the door swung open. I looked up to see Gail standing there with a curious look on her face. She closed the door behind her, walked straight to my desk, and put her hands on her hips.

"What?" I asked sheepishly, figuring I must have blown it somehow…again!

"Otis," she said. And now I knew this was serious; she usually calls me Honey. She went on, "If God ever calls you to Fresno—"

My head snapped upward and my whole body leaned toward her.

"—then let's go," she said.

At that moment you could have pushed me over with a feather. Gail knew nothing about what I had been wrestling with, but in her own heart God had confirmed His will for us. I knew I had heard from God, and God alone. We needed His guidance to be crystal-clear to both of us, and it was.

Now we could move forward on the move north with a confidence and certainty that sprang from the intimacy of fellowship with God in the secret place—and from knowing that the devil had no chance to thwart a plan he knew little about!

## Free from Doubts

Although dealing with God in the secret place makes His will clearer to us, it doesn't make His will any easier. For

Gail and me, it was as if a rug had been jerked out from under us. After enjoying a settledness for thirteen years, we now experienced confusion and bewilderment. We had some hard times ahead of us, some so difficult it might have prompted some serious second-guessing. But we were never plagued with doubts about whether we were in God's will in this move, because we could always look back and see how His plan had been made unquestionably clear in the secret place. His leading had been unmistakable.

Despite the many difficulties in this time of transition, the fruit of meeting with God in the secret place energized me to a new level of relationship with God that enriched my prayer life and infused my days with new purpose. For Gail and me, the secret place became ever more valuable in our continued search to understand our new circumstances and the new ministry directions in which the Lord was leading us.

*Chapter Five*

# OUR ENEMY
# SHUT OUT

*"The prince of this world....*
*has no hold on me."*
JOHN 14:30, NIV

You can be confident that the secret place we read about in
the Psalms is a place of refuge from the influence of Satan
and his subordinates. Although the devil's influence is per-
vasive in our world, God has placed boundaries on his
power that bar him from the secret place.

When I explain this to people, they often respond in
amazement: "You mean Satan can't read my thoughts?"

It's more than a pleasure for me to answer, "Even the
powers of darkness are locked out of your secret place. It's a

place of divine protection. Neither Satan nor his demons have access to it."

## SATAN DOESN'T KNOW OUR THOUGHTS

Unfortunately there's a common misconception—or perhaps I should say, a common deception—about the scope of our enemy's powers and abilities. He would have us believe that he knows everything we're thinking, that there's nothing we can hide from him. Our deception on that point needlessly allows him to discourage and intimidate us.

*There's never any indication in Scripture that the devil can know our thoughts.*

It's true, of course, that our thoughts aren't completely private. God Himself shows repeatedly in Scripture that He's aware of everything going on in our minds. "The LORD knows the thoughts of man" (Psalm 94:11); "All things are naked and open to the eyes of Him to whom we must give account" (Hebrews 4:13).

But there's never any indication in the Scriptures that the devil or his demons can know our thoughts, much as he would like us to think so. They can suggest and even manipulate our thinking through numerous influences, if we aren't on guard against them. But they're ultimately shut out from knowing exactly what anyone is silently thinking.

I've found that this truth is a freeing discovery for many believers, just as it was for me.

## Demonic Weakness Exposed

We see this truth played out in dramatic fashion in the book of Daniel. When King Nebuchadnezzar had a troubling dream and couldn't go back to sleep, he summoned his court magicians, astrologers, and sorcerers—definitely a crew you would expect to be in touch with demonic powers—to interpret his dream.

Dream interpretation was their specialty, so they respectfully responded with a reasonable request: "Tell your servants the dream, and we will give the interpretation" (Daniel 2:4). But the king decided to be unreasonable. To ensure a trustworthy analysis from a reliable source, he asked these men to first repeat to him exactly what he had dreamed. He promised "gifts, rewards, and great honor" if, along with an interpretation, they told him the vision the same way he dreamed it.

And if they didn't?

"You shall be cut in pieces," the king promised, "and your houses shall be made an ash heap" (2:5–6).

These guys were definitely motivated to come up with this private knowledge, by hook or by crook. But on this occasion at least, these conjurers were forced to be honest: They told the king he was asking the impossible. We can be assured that if somehow they could have tapped into their demonic connections to steal the contents of the king's dream, they would have sold their souls to do it. But instead they protested, "There is not a man on earth who can do what the king asks! No king, however great and mighty, has ever asked such a thing of any magician or enchanter or astrologer. What the king asks is too difficult" (2:10–11, NIV).

*They told the king he was asking the impossible.*

Furious, Nebuchadnezzar issued the order for his soldiers to execute all the wise men in his service. This would have included, unfortunately, Daniel and his three friends Shadrach, Meshach, and Abednego. Only divine intervention through Daniel saved their lives.

## DANIEL IN THE SECRET PLACE

When Daniel was told of the king's order and the reason for it, he went that night into the secret place to meet with his God. And there the contents of the king's dream, as well as their meaning, were revealed to him.

Daniel had earlier asked his three friends to pray urgently for God to show him this mystery. But once the dream was made known to him, we have no record of his letting his friends in on what God had revealed. We can easily imagine why.

Although Satan's forces cannot read our thoughts, they can listen in on our spoken words—and information is power. If a demon had overheard the interpretation explained by Daniel, he could easily have taken this information to the sorcerers or astrologers and let them become the hero in the presence of the king, while also enhancing demonic influence upon the king and his kingdom.

Instead, through Daniel's prudent wisdom, God Himself and God alone would get the glory.

When Daniel stood before Nebuchadnezzar, he confirmed that for anyone except God, getting inside the king's mind was impossible: "No wise man, enchanter, magician or diviner can explain to the king the mystery he has asked about, but there is a God in heaven who reveals mysteries" (2:27–28, NIV).

Daniel went on to relate the king's dream in striking detail, and added God's explanation of them, an interpretation that pointed to future events with sweeping, worldwide impact. Then the king "fell on his face, prostrate before Daniel" (v. 46). Besides bestowing on Daniel incredible gifts, honor, and authority, the king also gave glory where glory was most due: "Truly your God is the God of gods, the Lord of kings, and a revealer of secrets" (v. 47).

## Our Enemy—Limited and Defeated

It's a critical mistake to think Satan essentially has the same degree of power and knowledge God has, or even anything close to it. The very fact that God threw Satan and his followers out of heaven and doomed them to an eternity in hell proves that God's might is infinitely beyond our enemy's.

God wants us to understand that our enemy is already condemned and defeated. "The ruler of this world is judged," Jesus said (John 16:11). After being encouraged by a voice from His Father in heaven while drawing near to the hour of His crucifixion, Jesus announced, "Now the ruler of this world will be cast out" (John 12:31). The writer of Hebrews tells us that "through death" Jesus was able to "destroy him who had the power of death, that is, the devil" (Hebrews 2:14).

This victory by Jesus extends to the demonic hosts; on the cross and in His resurrection, Jesus "disarmed principalities and powers, He made a public spectacle of them, triumphing over them" (Colossians 2:15).

By the Lord's overwhelming power, our enemy is already a destroyed enemy, and that destruction will be made total and absolute in the future day described in Revelation 20:10. We ourselves have a share in that victory; as Paul tells us, "The God of peace will soon crush Satan under your feet" (Romans 16:20, NIV).

But even apart from this fatal blow against them at the hands of Christ, Satan and his demons have never been all-powerful or all-knowing or able to be in several places at once. And they never will be. As beings created by God (originally as

*Our enemy is already a destroyed enemy.*

———— ✿ ————

angels), they've always been restricted to being in only one location at a time. In fact, because Satan is limited this way, chances are great that neither you nor I have ever had any encounter with him.

## STILL PRESSURING THE WHOLE WORLD

But don't think that because Satan's presence is limited, so is his influence. A network of fallen angels are everywhere carrying out Satan's bidding so that, as John tells us, "the whole world lies under the sway of the wicked one" (1 John 5:19). We're confronted daily by the pressure of his forces.

In their intelligence-gathering for their warfare waged against us, these demons observe what's going on in our lives and draw all kinds of intelligent conclusions for devising their strategies against us.

They've become quite skilled at this. Ever since Satan watched Adam and Eve in the garden, he and his allies have had thousands of years to intricately study human nature. So don't be lulled into thinking that because he isn't all-knowing, he's therefore un-knowing. The devil's forces certainly know enough to attack where God appears to be most at work. They're always watching, listening, and gathering and sharing information. They're well acquainted with our frailty and defects, and they know how to leverage them against us with perfect timing.

Armed with such tactics, Satan's forces will try to thwart God's purpose in your life. The last thing they want for you or for any believer is a dynamic experience of God's presence in your secret place and the clear discovery of God's will that comes there. They'll do all they can to discourage you in this, since they're shut out from observing what happens inside your secret place.

Author and Bible teacher Randy Alcorn pictures the evil one's influence and limitations this way:

> He can bang on the door and yell in the window and shout his accusations, but he can't invade the premises of my mind…because the Holy Spirit is in residence.
>
> But of course, we must be on the alert to wage war that demolishes Satan's arguments, and we must not be unaware of his strategies. We don't want to overestimate the power of demons in our lives, but neither do we want to underestimate it.

## How We Wisely Resist Our Enemy

To help us grasp the widespread dangers of Satan and his subordinates, Peter tells us bluntly, "Your adversary the devil walks about like a roaring lion, seeking whom he may devour." But don't let this fact discourage you. Immediately Peter exhorts us boldly, "Resist him, steadfast in the faith" (1 Peter 5:8–9). Those words echo the confident command we hear from James: "Resist the devil and he will flee from you" (James 4:7).

And how is such resistance possible, since the demons, despite their limitations, still seem plenty able to outsmart you or me? We can resist him because of God's living presence within us, according to the promise we read in John: "He who is in you is greater than he who is in the world" (1 John 4:4). God truly is infinitely

*We must stay cautious and informed about Satan's strategies.*

greater than the devil, and we make the most of that truth when we allow the Lord to focus and guide our lives through time spent alone with Him in the secret place.

We can therefore be confident in our continuing and unavoidable confrontations with the forces of evil, but we must also stay cautious and informed about Satan's strategies. "We are not ignorant of his devices"—that's the standard Paul sets forth, "lest Satan should take advantage of us" (2 Corinthians 2:11).

## Be Careful What You Say

Doesn't it make sense that if our life is the kind of spiritual battle portrayed in the Bible—where we're warned "to stand against the wiles of the devil," and told that we must actually "wrestle...against principalities, against powers, against the rulers of the darkness of this age, against spiritual hosts of wickedness in the heavenly places" (Ephesians 6:11–12)—then shouldn't our battle strategy include keeping as much vital information away from our sworn enemy as we possibly can?

But when we believe Satan knows all our thoughts anyway, we're far more likely to be careless in what we speak and to foolishly reveal information to Satan's forces that they can use to work evil in our lives or in the lives of our loved ones—information that should be kept between God and us.

Are you aware enough of Satan's devices to be protective of what you openly speak about—and to cover with protective prayer all the plans and goals and issues that you do speak openly about?

Failures in this area probably happen every day, contributing to the spiritual shipwrecks the devil brings about in so many believers' lives. When we speak too freely and carelessly about what God has communicated to us about our hopes and plans, the devil hears, and we make it easy for him to try to confuse God's clear leading in our lives. Our enemy will then do all he can to bring our pride to the surface, so we'll rely on ourselves rather than on the Spirit and on prayer.

## GIVING AMMO TO THE ENEMY

After I gave a message on the secret place at a men's retreat I attended in Idaho, another man spoke to the group about his chronic battle with depression. "I tried everything to bring myself out of that pit, but nothing worked. I found myself constantly complaining to my wife and anyone else who would listen about the funk I found myself in."

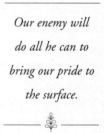

*Our enemy will do all he can to bring our pride to the surface.*

Finally, he said, "I decided to just not talk about it anymore, so I quit. To my surprise it slowly went away."

He looked over the audience of men and added, "I've never thought about it before today, but now I know why. I was giving the evil one plenty of ammo. When I stopped…the depression stopped!"

## UNDERMINING YOUR OWN MARRIAGE

Lori came to my office one day and told me that things weren't going well between her and her husband, Sean. This surprised me, because they hadn't been married long.

I asked her how she thought the problems began.

"I'm not really sure," she responded. "It came on pretty suddenly."

"Well, let's go back as far as you can remember," I suggested.

Lori remembered becoming unhappy with some of Sean's personal mannerisms. There was no great misstep or betrayal on his part; it seemed obvious to me that Lori was just experiencing the simple disillusionment that happens when a marriage doesn't meet a certain level of expectation.

As her disappointments began to build, Lori said she sought out a friend in her Bible class named Michelle and began to openly reveal how the disappointments were affecting her. She made statements to Michelle like these:

"It makes me want to move back home with my parents."

"Maybe I married the wrong person."

"It pushes me closer to this guy at work."

If Lori's thoughts and actions sound harmless, perhaps that's part of the deception from the evil one. By carelessly confessing such feelings, she may well have been exposing weaknesses that could easily be seized upon by the enemy—and turned into a strategy against her leading to something disastrous in their marriage.

Lori's feelings might be normal, but instead of spilling them out verbally, she would have been wiser to take her cares to God in the secret place, seeking His help by faith in living a Spirit-led life and enjoying His fulfillment and protection.

As I explained to Lori this principle of the secret place, her eyes widened and her mouth dropped open. She realized she was giving private information into the hands of the enemy. She stopped carelessly discussing her feelings and began seeking answers and comfort in the Lord through the security of her secret place with Him. It has saved her and Sean from what I believe could have been heartbreak in their future.

*She would have been wiser to take her cares to God in the secret place.*

This isn't to say that it's wrong to seek counsel, or even to confess our sins to others. But openly revealing feelings and frustrations can sometimes provide the tools of tragedy that Satan's forces can use against us. In times of personal distress and need, the best advice you can get is to go and meet with God in the secret place. There, God can help you formulate a plan. He can help you understand and sort out your feelings. And He can do it before Satan can use them for any mischief in your life.

## WAITING FOR THE RIGHT TIME TO TALK

Gail and I have come to believe so intently in experiencing God's presence in the secret place, and have grown so accustomed to doing business with Him in this way, that it's usually apparent when one of us is working on some major issue there with God.

One evening a few weeks ago, I was lying on the couch after a particularly eventful day. Normally I'll detail my day to my wife so she can share in my triumphs and defeats, but that evening I was evidently far away mentally. As Gail brought out a tray with the evening meal she'd prepared and set it on the ottoman in front of me, she asked if anything was wrong. I shook my head.

"Are you in the secret place?" she asked.

"Yes," I replied.

She immediately understood what was happening and didn't press the matter. It gave her an opportunity to effectively pray for my progress and wisdom in the matter God and I were discussing.

We have both learned that there's a proper time to share more details with one another, so that waiting for and anticipating that moment becomes a pleasure, not an irritant.

## MIGHTY WEAPONS IN GOD

When it comes to the life-issues and spiritual matters you discuss with those who are close to you, there simply is no more effective way to protect them and to fully resist the devil's opposition than to enlist God's power through prayer against him.

That's what Jesus Himself did on Simon Peter's behalf; "Indeed," Jesus told him, "Satan has asked for you, that he may sift you as wheat. But I have prayed for you, that your faith should not fail" (Luke 22:31–32).

When Paul warns us to stand against the devil's schemes by putting on God's full armor, he goes on to show us how to accomplish this—by "praying always with all prayer and supplication in the Spirit, being watchful to this end with all perseverance and supplication for all the saints" (Ephesians 6:18).

> *Our warfare with Satan's forces is not like human warfare.*

Our warfare with Satan's forces is not like human warfare; as Paul says, "though we walk in the flesh, we do not war according to the flesh. For the weapons of our warfare are not carnal but mighty in God for pulling down strongholds" (2 Corinthians 10:3–4).

The battle is spiritual, and prayer is the comprehensive spiritual weapon. Prayer coverage—prayer in the secret place, and prayer all day long—is the proof of your genuine dependence on God.

*Chapter Six*

# FINDING YOUR FUTURE

*Commit your works to the LORD,*
*and your thoughts will be established.*
PROVERBS 16:3

In the secret place, God is waiting. He's fully prepared to guide and inspire men and women in their plans and dreams, and He's there to show them renewed and expanded life-pursuits and vocations…resulting in fresh new ventures and ministries and churches that together will literally bless the entire world.

The question is: What will your God-given part be in all this?

You'll find the answer to that question unfolding in the intimacy of the secret place, where the God who created all things will funnel His power and His will to you. Wherever you may be now in service for God's kingdom, your impact will only be enhanced and strengthened by allowing Him to clarify and fortify your work and purpose and goals.

*You can safely pursue plans and dreams while being insulated from criticism.*

In God's presence within the secret place, you can safely pursue thoughts and plans and dreams while being insulated from any criticism from those around you and being free from the world's distractions. He'll make plain to you how His Word applies to your specific circumstances now and in your future.

Within this nurturing environment of intimate fellowship with your Creator and Lord, His purpose and plans for your life can safely mature in your heart and mind as you and God do business together. You can carefully sort these plans out, strategize them, and lay the groundwork for implementing them in your life.

## WHERE MINISTRY IMPACT BEGINS

When we hear the stories of ministry pioneers of the past, we recognize how their time spent alone in God's presence nurtured the vision and guidance and endurance they needed to push ahead with their calling. Ministries that have a global impact today were at one time nothing more than a dream conceived in one person's secret place. The God who gave birth to those dreams also nurtured them into realities.

As I mentioned earlier, for thirteen years, Gail and I were established in successful ministries through our church and a Christian college in Southern California. God had to move us from the familiar to the unfamiliar to focus us on something new He planned for us. In that process, He led us to two couples who had the same passion for strengthening the family that Gail and I shared. Through more time spent in the secret place, the Heritage Builders Association was birthed. Today, HBA is touching families around the world as a part of another organization—Focus on the Family—that also was birthed from time in the secret place. Their founder, Dr. James Dobson, testifies that the roots of Focus on the Family go back to his father's intimacy with God.

I want to encourage you to enter the secret place and obtain God's help in rethinking your old plans and attitudes and assumptions, and initiating new ones. Pull out all the stops in the process of being "transformed by the renewing of your mind, that you may prove what is that good and acceptable and perfect will of God" (Romans 12:2).

## It Isn't Automatic

But be aware that genuinely hearing and understanding God's true will for your life, as He reveals it in the secret place, doesn't happen automatically.

Many times I hear people wish that God would more clearly vocalize His will to them. Perhaps He is clearly vocalizing it, but we're looking for His will to be revealed through some ecstatic supernatural experience instead of through His quiet promptings. Or perhaps we're simply distracted by having too much clutter in our lives—what I call "life-litter."

As we trudge through life's daily trials, sometimes our spirits get cluttered by cynicism and doubt and weariness. Life's routine dissipates our patience, shortens our perseverance, and dulls our ability to clearly perceive what's happening.

It's like what happened to my computer. A few days ago I noticed it was operating a little slowly. Of course in these days of instant everything, if the computer delays five seconds, it seems like an eternity. My computer-savvy son-in-law noticed my frustration, checked out my computer, and informed me that it had accumulated too many temporary Internet files—files from those places I'd visited on the Internet. My machine was so slow because it was bogged down with useless information from the past. As soon as we dumped those old files that were taking up vital memory, the computer gained new life and began to perk up.

Our responses to life's predicaments and challenges can build up the same kind of accumulation inside us, stuffing the storage capacity of our spirits with lingering anxieties. The hurts and disappointments we undergo are especially potent in cramming us inside with wounded pride, self-pity, vindictiveness, defeatism, and other spirit-consuming responses. Our spiritual vitality gets trampled. Our effectiveness in God's kingdom bogs down.

## GETTING UNCLOGGED

You and I were never meant to be a debris pile for collecting and living under our accumulated cares, overloaded with life's useless baggage. How then do we dig out from under the pile?

By "casting all your care upon Him, for He cares for you" (1 Peter 5:7). David told us this as well: "Cast your burden on the LORD, and He shall sustain you" (Psalm 55:22).

*How then do we dig out from under the pile?*

This casting is an activity that happens best in the secret place.

What is it in your life right now that needs to be cast on the Lord in order for you to freely live the abundant life He has called you to? Whatever it is, hurry to the secret place and do this urgent business with God.

*Chapter Seven*

❦

# WAITING ON GOD

*I wait for the LORD, my soul waits,
and in His word I do hope.*
PSALM 130:5

God waits in our secret place all the time, every day. He's never absent. To help us discover His will for us, He waits there for us to rendezvous with Him—something we're sometimes willing to do only after we've tried everything else.

And one of the things we often try is the "fleece" method of finding God's will, especially in understanding His timing for our planned actions. It's something I've used, and most everyone I've talked with about it has at one time or another "put out the fleece."

But is it a good way to go about finding God's leading? And if it isn't—why isn't it?

## Gideon's Experience

You remember the story.

Gideon, who was the least member of the least clan in his nation, was appointed by God to lead his people out from under the oppressive iron grip of the powerful Midianites.

As the decisive battle approached, Gideon longed for the confidence that God was indeed with Israel, and to make sure, he decided to use a simple fleece of wool. He laid it on the ground outside his tent, and made his request to the Lord—that in the morning, God would make the fleece wet and the ground around it dry.

The next morning, Gideon rose early. The ground was dry, but he squeezed a bowlful of dew from the fleece. God had honored his request.

Gideon then pleaded for yet another sign on the next night as well, again using the fleece: "Let it now be dry only on the fleece, but on all the ground let there be dew" (Judges 6:39).

The next morning, he discovered that God had again answered his request, and Gideon was satisfied.

## So Tempting

Obviously, the fleece worked well for Gideon. Down through the ages people have read his story, marveled at the simplicity of it, and tried to duplicate its success. It promises to take the guesswork out of discerning God's direction for our lives.

In my opinion, however, relying on a fleece is a dangerous mistake. It's an attempted shortcut for people who want instant results instead of being committed enough to develop a confident, personal understanding of God's will. When the Lord seems to be moving too slowly in guiding

> *Relying on a fleece is a dangerous mistake.*

us, or His will doesn't seem clear, the fleece is such a tempting substitute for patience.

I've heard people testify that the fleece worked for them. But how do we really know it wasn't sheer coincidence or self-fulfilling prophecies? Or for that matter, how do we know it wasn't a set of circumstances orchestrated by the evil one?

## RED DRESS, GREEN DRESS

Bobby was a young man I went to school with in Sherman, Texas. His athletic ability made him very popular. He came to the Lord after his senior year in high school and started attending the same church I did. His spiritual growth was impressive, and he followed the Lord as fiercely as he had pursued sports. He taught a children's class at church and also began reaching out to his former teammates, leading many to Christ. His passion for Jesus was so enthusiastic that many people in our church could easily envision the day Bobby would become a preacher.

One Sunday morning he gave a testimony about his future. He announced that he had surrendered to full-time Christian ministry, and applause broke out that lasted for what seemed like several minutes. But the enthusiasm of his audience quickly mellowed as Bobby went on with his story.

He told the church how hearing the sermon a few weeks earlier on Gideon and the fleece had inspired him to confirm a calling he'd sensed. "I wasn't sure if God really was asking me to do this or not," he admitted.

"Then Thursday morning I noticed a lady standing at the bus stop in front of my business wearing a red dress. I've been wondering what God wanted me to do." Bobby paused, bowed his head, then raised his eyes as if looking out at us over invisible reading glasses. "So Thursday night during our family prayer time, I told God and my family that if He wanted me in ministry, to have a lady standing there at the bus stop in a green dress in the morning."

With his jaw squared, he quickly finished: "Sure enough, the next morning, there she stood in a green skirt. So here I am this morning, keeping my end of the bargain."

I knew Bobby personally. It wasn't my place to judge him, and he wasn't one to lie or fabricate a story. He seemed to truly trust the fleece for a while. But because the fleece was used as a shortcut around a clear, personal discernment of God's will, he later began to doubt the authenticity of his call.

Unfortunately the end of this story isn't a happy one. Bobby's ministry from that day forward was plagued with uncertainty, second guesses, and questions about what exactly God was doing. Finally he surrendered his calling altogether. He quit bringing people to church and grew embittered toward God. His entire spiritual life lay in ruin.

*The fleece was used as a shortcut around personal discernment of God's will.*

I heard Bobby complain one day that he wished God "would never have put that lady on that street corner that morning." Today, Bobby doesn't even attend church because he feels God betrayed him.

For whatever it's worth, I'm not sure God put that lady there. And, tragically, neither is Bobby.

Maybe it wasn't just Bobby's family that heard his request that night about the green dress. Maybe the enemy was there and heard it too. It's possible that the enemy, for the purpose of laying in Bobby's heart a foundation for doubt and bitterness that would later afflict him, suggested wearing a green dress to an unsuspecting lady choosing her wardrobe that particular morning. It's possible the enemy was using the information he overheard to manipulate circumstances to make it appear God was saying something He wasn't.

## A Game Our Enemy Likes to Play

You may be thinking I've chosen an extreme case to illustrate this point. Or you might assume that Satan's limitations would keep him from ever manufacturing any "sign" that we ask for only from God. But from what we see happening with Moses and Aaron as they stood before Pharaoh, this seems to be exactly the kind of game the devil likes to play.

*This is the kind of game the devil likes to play.*

Pharaoh asked Moses and Aaron to perform a miracle; then Aaron, under God's instructions, threw down his rod and it became a serpent. But Pharaoh called in his own sorcerers and magicians, and they did the same thing, most likely by demonic influence. When Aaron later used his rod to turn Egypt's water into blood and to cover the land with frogs, Pharaoh's conjurers again made a show of reproducing both acts (although, with unbloody water hard to find at that point and frogs already everywhere, perhaps this wasn't so impressive after all).

If "Satan himself transforms himself into an angel of light" (2 Corinthians 11:14), deceptive tricks like that are only to be expected from his forces still today.

## Risky Business

Consider again those two stories—Gideon's and Bobby's. The fleece worked for one, but not for the other. That should lead us to a clear conclusion: The fleece is risky business at best. It lends itself to second-guessing one's actions after it's too late, and far too many "fleeces" lead only to disappointment and disillusionment.

The important point to keep in mind here is that our clear understanding of God's will in our life is a serious threat to Satan. To keep us from knowing it, he'll try everything—including imitating providential signs in order to deceive us. It's a sobering truth to realize Satan can mimic God's power of God and fabricate a set of circumstances for those who would publicly use a fleece to determine God's will. The "signs" they receive after asking God to show them may actually be Satan's counterfeit.

## Something Better

For getting a "go" sign from God, there has to be a better approach than the fleece, one that isn't so fraught with inherent uncertainties.

And there is—the secret place. That should be our first

destination when we need guidance from our Father. It's there we can pour out our heart and find answers, in the presence of the One who works everything for our good. Shielded there from our enemy, we'll find refreshing strength and wisdom, in the certainty that the plans made with God in the confidentiality of our secret place can't be co-opted by Satan's cronies.

Relying on the secret place instead of attempting short-cuts to finding God's will would help prevent tragic stories like Bobby's.

Some Christians bemoan how "difficult" it is to find God's will. I think I understand the heart of someone who entertains that notion, but in hindsight I've always found His answers to be on time and apparent. They haven't always been to my liking, but they've always been true to His written Word.

## MONEY FOR A PHONE CALL

Years ago a young woman in our church approached me after I'd spoken on this subject to tell me about something that had happened in her life. As she began, I first thought she was relating another "fleece" story. But as she continued, I sensed her genuine interest in doing business alone with God through the mystery and intimacy of the secret place.

"I'd been dating this guy my parents didn't approve of,"

she said. "Since I'm over twenty, I
figured I knew what was best. I was
blinded by love. But I heard you say
in a sermon that the devil couldn't
read my thoughts and that I should
do business in the secret place, so I
took you up on it."

*I sensed her
genuine interest in
doing business
alone with God.*

She pondered her parents' objec-
tions to this relationship, then decided to take it to the Lord
in her secret place. She came up with a plan known only to
her and to God.

She was at college, and to break off the relationship
would require a long-distance phone call—something she
couldn't afford at the time. She felt that asking her parents
for the money would violate the spirit of her plan. Instead,
she asked God to give her the extra money required.
Otherwise she would have to resign herself to waiting for
the next time her boyfriend phoned her.

She had a job that barely gave her enough spending
money while in school. She worked at a smorgasbord-style
cafeteria, where customers rarely gave tips to those doing
what she did—busing tables. But a nice tip, she thought,
would probably be enough to pay for the call.

As she related what happened when she next went to
work after making her plans with God, she almost shouted:
"Can you imagine how my heart jumped? For the first time

on my job people left money on the tables! I can't remember that happening again during the eight months I worked there."

She made the phone call that night and ended the relationship. Soon, God brought an outstanding young man into her life. They're now pastoring a church, and she's even authored a couple of books.

# Chapter Eight

# SHINING A BRIGHTER LIGHT

*Now you are light in the Lord.*
EPHESIANS 5:8

It's our command from Jesus: "Let your light so shine before men, that they may see your good works and glorify your Father in heaven" (Matthew 5:16).

We're to be lights in this world. And as we carry on our good works, what is it that will make us shine? What will draw the attention of others, in the positive way that Jesus is speaking about? Is it our own goodness?

Hardly. Rather, it's the Lord's own presence and personality reflected in and through us—and that's something that comes only from our intimate contact with Him.

After Moses came down from meeting alone with God on Mount Sinai, the Scriptures tell us his face glowed—so brightly that he used to wear a veil to cover it. That glow was the fruit of his intimate contact with God.

That's the source of true light in us as well. And our glow will keep getting brighter with ever-increasing intimacy in our fellowship with God in the secret place:

More time there with Him is how we "put on the armor of light" (Romans 13:12).

*If you want to revolutionize your witness, pursue a deeper intimacy with God in the secret place.*

It's how we learn to "walk as children of light" (Ephesians 5:8).

It's how we're able to "shine as lights in the world" (Philippians 2:15).

The radiance of the Spirit's love, joy, and peace, kindled and fanned into flame in our secret place, can't help but be noticed in the darkness of this world and will draw others toward Him.

If you want to revolutionize the impact of your witness in your world, pursuing a deeper intimacy with God in the secret place is where to start.

## Too Time-Demanding?

But some resist the idea of the secret place because it seems to demand too much time. In our fast-paced world, we want instant help and answers from God more than a growing relationship and dependence that's nurtured in the secret place. We want instant impact and influence in others' lives and instant improvement in our own. We want God's blessings, and we want them *now!*

The secret place has no room for such impatience because the secret place is timeless. The plans being shaped there, the answers being clarified, and the lessons being learned have connections to the eternal and are far too important for deadlines. There are no fast computers there. Don't expect a drive-through window. There's no remote with appropriate buttons to push to manipulate life's channels.

No, none of what's being accomplished in this place can be served up instantly. In the secret place, in fact, the actual timing of God's answers is as delightful and pleasing and helpful as the answers themselves, even if the answer is *Wait.*

## TOO DISRESPECTFUL?

Other believers resist the concept of the secret place on a different level. To them, attempting such intimacy with God is too disrespectful or irreverent. That's the objection that Charles Wesley reportedly heard when he was criticized for his hymn "Jesus, Lover of My Soul."

But the Bible teaches that such intimacy is both real

and priceless. It's also mysterious; when Paul speaks of a man joining his wife so that "the two shall become one flesh," he adds: "This is a great mystery, but I speak concerning Christ and the church" (Ephesians 5:31–32). We're the bride of Christ, and our relational intensity with Him is illustrated by the spontaneous, ecstatic, and protective love between man and woman as portrayed in the Song of Solomon.

This intimacy with God is spiritual, but the Bible uses our physical senses to portray it, helping us understand better the relationship He wants with us:

"Oh, taste and see that the LORD is good" (Psalm 34:8).

"O God, You are my God…my soul thirsts for You; my flesh longs for You" (Psalm 63:1).

"Incline your ear, and come to Me. Hear, and your soul shall live" (Isaiah 55:3).

Such intimacy with God ensures a relationship that never tires of closeness. You'll want to keep returning to the secret place again and again as you grow in true intimacy with Him; there'll be no such thing there as getting bored or disinterested.

## THE UNIMAGINABLE

What will this intimacy lead to? Because God is limitless in love and power and majesty and all His attributes, there's no limit to what He's able to reveal about Himself to you over time, as He so wills. Consider, for example, what He chose to reveal to the beloved apostle John.

The last book of the New Testament begins with John in the secret place. On a certain Sunday ("the Lord's day") on the island of Patmos, the aged apostle was "in the Spirit" (Revelation 1:10)—in the secret place. If we had been standing nearby, the amazing things John saw that day would not have been visible to us; the astonishing things he heard would have been outside our hearing.

But because John was immediately commanded to write down what he saw and heard, we as well now have the privilege of seeing and hearing those things. And when we

> *There's no limit to what He's able to reveal about Himself to you over time.*

do, we realize what an overpowering perspective he was given of the Lord Jesus Christ in all His terrifying majesty and victorious might and tender mercy—the King of kings and Lord of lords, consummating His reign over all creation and bringing to an utter end the devil and his followers and all the evil and deceit they've inspired over the ages, then forever fulfilling the deepest needs of His chosen ones.

What can God reveal to you in His secret place? It's unimaginable; it's what "eye has not seen, nor ear heard";

treasures that are inconceivable to our minds and hearts are the very things "which God has prepared for those who love Him," and which He reveals to us "through His Spirit" (1 Corinthians 2:9–10), just as He did for John on Patmos.

And as you experience those treasures, your influence in this world will break forth in new dimensions.

## Your Secret Garden

In Frances Hodgson Burnett's children's classic *The Secret Garden,* the young orphan Mary Lennox is sent to live with distant family members. Their large, dreary house seems haunted, and the family deeply depressed.

In time, Mary's intense curiosity leads her to knowledge about a locked-away garden that had once been a hub of happiness for the family; the father would retire regularly there with his wife. But ever since her death, his anger and bitterness has kept him away. Even the thought of being there is repulsive to him.

Mary can't stand such lingering despair and sets out to change things. She finds the key to the garden and locates the door. She unlocks it and enters, finding the once beautiful garden overgrown and ugly. It isn't an inviting place at all, but her realization that it once had been priceless drives her to labor. She helps restore the garden to its original beauty; the barren earth is transformed into a world of splendor.

Rediscovering the garden's magic and unlocking its mysteries brings back happiness to everyone involved. The story ends with the father standing in his restored former sanctuary, wishing he had never abandoned his secret garden.

*She couldn't stand such lingering despair and set out to change things.*

It's my highest hope that you'll rediscover your own secret place. Even if you find it weed-filled from neglect and disinterest, be assured that God is waiting for you there to restore the place where He does His best work in your life.

Go there today and start a new level of intimacy with God that can transform your life and even change our world.

The key has been found.

The door has been unlocked.

Right now…He's waiting there for you!

*Chapter 9*

# GOD'S PROMISES TO EXPLORE IN THE SECRET PLACE

*But you, when you pray, go into your room, and when you have*
*shut your door, pray to your Father who is in the secret place;*
*and your Father who sees in secret will reward you openly.*
MATTHEW 6:6

When we look at how God operates through the Old and
New Testaments, we find that He's always reserving something for Himself. He holds something back and marks it
in a special way as belonging to Him alone. In the Garden
of Eden, it was a tree located in the center of it. In the
Tabernacle and later in the Temple, it was the innermost

Holy of Holies. Among the peoples and nations of the world, it was the Jews, and later the Church. In the flow of His people's income and productivity, it was the tithe.

When it comes to an individual man or woman, there's also something God has reserved for Himself. It's where the Creator meets with His creation; it's a place within each believer where the Most High alone has the right to enter.

Waiting for you now, in that intimate setting marked "Reserved," are unique experiences with God your Father that are yours to hold and treasure forever.

*There's something God has reserved for Himself.*

As we've seen, it's more than a place of physical safety and more than a place of spiritual rest. It's a place where you discern and discover the Lord's clear guidance through the illumination of His Word…where silent, secret plans for your life can begin and be energized…where fragile ideas are free to mature…where you're enabled to face the challenges ahead of you in life with renewed vigor…where you find answers to life's most perplexing and dangerous situations…where you find trustworthy sign-markers for every crossroads in your life.

Above all, it's the place where you enjoy your deepest and most personal fellowship with the Almighty.

Ignited by the Holy Spirit's fire, the Word of the Lord will come to you there through the pages of Scripture. In His inspired writings you'll encounter authentic truth about who He is, who you are, and what your life in Him is meant to be.

Filling the rest of this chapter are promises from those sacred pages that I encourage you to return to often.

## FOR INTIMACY WITH GOD

Draw near to God and He will draw near to you.

JAMES 4:8

I will be a Father to you, and you shall be My sons and daughters, says the LORD Almighty.

2 CORINTHIANS 6:18

Beloved, now we are children of God.

1 JOHN 3:2

The love of God has been poured out in our hearts by the Holy Spirit who was given to us.

ROMANS 5:5

Behold, I stand at the door and knock.
If anyone hears My voice and opens the door, I will come in to him and dine with him, and he with Me.

REVELATION 3:20

If anyone loves Me, he will keep My word;
and My Father will love him,
and We will come to him and make Our home with him.

John 14:23

If you keep My commandments,
you will abide in My love, just as I have kept
My Father's commandments and abide in His love.

John 15:10

The Lord your God in your midst,
The Mighty One, will save;
He will rejoice over you with gladness,
He will quiet you with His love,
He will rejoice over you with singing."

Zephaniah 3:17

I am with you always, even to the end of the age.

Matthew 28:20

FOR WISDOM AND UNDERSTANDING

For with You is the fountain of life;
In Your light we see light.

Psalm 36:9

I will put My laws in their mind and
write them on their hearts; and I will be their God,
and they shall be My people.

Hebrews 8:10


For you were once darkness,
but now you are light in the Lord.

Ephesians 5:8


The darkness is passing away,
and the true light is already shining.

1 John 2:8


For You are my lamp, O Lord;
The Lord shall enlighten my darkness.

2 Samuel 22:29


And we know that the Son of God has come and has
given us an understanding....

1 John 5:20


The Helper, the Holy Spirit, whom the Father will send
in My name, He will teach you all things, and bring to
your remembrance all things that I said to you.

John 14:26

If any of you lacks wisdom, let him ask of God,
who gives to all liberally and without reproach,
and it will be given to him.

JAMES 1:5

Therefore let us, as many as are mature, have this mind;
and if in anything you think otherwise,
God will reveal even this to you.

PHILIPPIANS 3:15

## FOR GUIDANCE

The sheep hear his voice; and he calls his own
sheep by name and leads them out.

JOHN 10:3

My sheep hear My voice, and I know them,
and they follow Me.

JOHN 10:27

I will instruct you and teach you
in the way you should go.
I will guide you with My eye.

PSALM 32:8

In all your ways acknowledge Him,
And He shall direct your paths.

Proverbs 3:6


I am the light of the world.
He who follows Me shall not walk in darkness,
but have the light of life.

John 8:12


I will put My Spirit within you and
cause you to walk in My statutes,
and you will keep My judgments and do them.

Ezekiel 36:27


## FOR LIFE STRATEGIES AND PLANS

You will show me the path of life.

Psalm 16:11


The LORD shall preserve your going out and your coming
in from this time forth, and even forevermore.

Psalm 121:8


Then you will walk safely in your way,
And your foot will not stumble.

Proverbs 3:23

He who has begun a good work in you will
complete it until the day of Jesus Christ.

PHILIPPIANS 1:6


But the path of the just is like the shining sun,
That shines ever brighter unto the perfect day.

PROVERBS 4:18


For the LORD God is a sun and shield;
The LORD will give grace and glory;
No good thing will He withhold
From those who walk uprightly.

PSALM 84:11


And my God shall supply all your need according
to His riches in glory by Christ Jesus.

PHILIPPIANS 4:19


Ask, and it will be given to you; seek, and you will find;
knock, and it will be opened to you.
For everyone who asks receives,
and he who seeks finds,
and to him who knocks it will be opened.

MATTHEW 7:7-8

If you abide in My word, you are My disciples indeed.
And you shall know the truth,
and the truth shall make you free.

John 8:31–32

Now the Lord is the Spirit;
and where the Spirit of the Lord is, there is liberty.

2 Corinthians 3:17

FOR WAITING ON GOD

The Lord is good to those who wait for Him,
To the soul who seeks Him.
It is good that one should hope and wait quietly
For the salvation of the Lord.

Lamentations 3:25–26

Wait for the Lord, and He will save you.

Proverbs 20:22

Wait on the Lord;
Be of good courage,
And He shall strengthen your heart;
Wait, I say, on the Lord!

Psalm 27:14

## IN TIMES OF TROUBLE

For in the time of trouble
He shall hide me in His pavilion;
In the secret place of His tabernacle
He shall hide me;
He shall set me high upon a rock.

PSALM 27:5


You are my hiding place;
You shall preserve me from trouble;
You shall surround me with songs of deliverance.

PSALM 32:7


In the shadow of Your wings I will make my refuge,
Until these calamities have passed by.

PSALM 57:1


He shall call upon Me, and I will answer him;
I will be with him in trouble;
I will deliver him and honor him.

PSALM 91:15

## FOR PEACE AND CALMNESS

Come to Me, all you who labor and are heavy laden,
and I will give you rest.

MATTHEW 11:28

Be anxious for nothing, but in everything by prayer
and supplication, with thanksgiving,
let your requests be made known to God;
and the peace of God, which surpasses all understanding,
will guard your hearts and minds through Christ Jesus.

PHILIPPIANS 4:6–7

We know that all things work together for good
to those who love God, to those who are
the called according to His purpose.

ROMANS 8:28

## FOR SPIRITUAL PROTECTION AND VICTORY

Therefore submit to God.
Resist the devil and he will flee from you.

JAMES 4:7

The God of peace will crush Satan under your feet.

ROMANS 16:20

He who dwells in the secret place of the Most High
Shall abide under the shadow of the Almighty.
I will say of the LORD,
"He is my refuge and my fortress;
My God, in Him I will trust."
Surely He shall deliver you from the snare of the fowler
And from the perilous pestilence.
He shall cover you with His feathers,
And under His wings you shall take refuge;
His truth shall be your shield and buckler.
You shall not be afraid of the terror by night,
Nor of the arrow that flies by day,
Nor of the pestilence that walks in darkness,
Nor of the destruction that lays waste at noonday.

PSALM 91:1–6


Oh, how great is Your goodness,
Which You have laid up for those who fear You,
Which You have prepared for those who trust in You
In the presence of the sons of men!
You shall hide them in the secret place of Your presence
From the plots of man;
You shall keep them secretly in a pavilion
From the strife of tongues.

PSALM 31:19–20

Do not rejoice over me, my enemy;
When I fall, I will arise;
When I sit in darkness,
The LORD will be a light to me.

MICAH 7:8

The Lord is faithful, who will establish you
and guard you from the evil one.

2 THESSALONIANS 3:3

The LORD shall preserve you from all evil;
He shall preserve your soul.

PSALM 121:7

If God is for us, who can be against us?

ROMANS 8:31

FOR STRENGTH AND ENCOURAGEMENT

Those who wait on the LORD
Shall renew their strength;
They shall mount up with wings like eagles,
They shall run and not be weary,
They shall walk and not faint.

ISAIAH 40:31

He Himself has said,
"I will never leave you nor forsake you."

HEBREWS 13:5


The LORD is my light and my salvation;
Whom shall I fear?
The LORD is the strength of my life;
Of whom shall I be afraid?

PSALM 27:1


## FOR GROWTH IN RIGHTEOUSNESS AND HOLINESS

Sin shall not have dominion over you,
for you are not under law but under grace.

ROMANS 6:14


Our Lord Jesus Christ…
will also confirm you to the end,
that you may be blameless in the day
of our Lord Jesus Christ.

1 CORINTHIANS 1:7–8


For this is the will of God, your sanctification.

1 THESSALONIANS 4:3

If we walk in the light as He is in the light…the blood of
Jesus Christ His Son cleanses us from all sin.… If we
confess our sins, He is faithful and just to forgive us our
sins and to cleanse us from all unrighteousness.

1 John 1:7,9

## SCRIPTURES TO PRAY FOR
## OTHERS IN THE SECRET PLACE

May the Lord give you understanding in all things.

2 Timothy 2:7

…making mention of you in my prayers:
that the God of our Lord Jesus Christ,
the Father of glory, may give to you the spirit of wisdom
and revelation in the knowledge of Him.

Ephesians 1:16–17

We also…do not cease to pray for you, and to ask that
you may be filled with the knowledge of His will in all
wisdom and spiritual understanding.

Colossians 1:9

The publisher and author would love to hear your comments about this book. *Please contact us at:*
www.multnomah.net/jotisledbetter

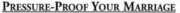

# BIG CHANGE

## PRESSURE-PROOF YOUR MARRIAGE
Family First Series, #3
**DENNIS & BARBARA RAINEY** ISBN 1-59052-211-7

Dennis and Barbara Rainey show you how to use pressure to your benefit, building intimacy with each other and with the Lord.

## TWO HEARTS PRAYING AS ONE
Family First Series, #2
**DENNIS & BARBARA RAINEY** ISBN 1-59052-035-1

Praying together daily is the best thing you can do for your marriage. Start right away with Dennis and Barbara Rainey's interactive guide!

## GROWING A SPIRITUALLY STRONG FAMILY
Family First Series, #1
**DENNIS & BARBARA RAINEY** ISBN 1-57673-778-0

Down-to-earth advice, encouraging stories, timely insights, and life-changing truths from FamilyLife's Dennis and Barbara Rainey direct parents on the path to leaving a godly family legacy.

## WRESTLING WITH GOD
Prayer That Never Gives Up
**GREG LAURIE** ISBN 1-59052-044-0

You struggle with God in your own unique way. See how your struggle can result in the most rewarding relationship with Him!

SMALL BOOKS
BIG CHANGE

# BIG CHANGE

## THE PURITY PRINCIPLE
God's Safeguards for Life's Dangerous Trails
**RANDY ALCORN** ISBN 1-59052-195-1

God has placed warning signs and guardrails to keep us from plunging off the cliff. Find straight talk about sexual purity in Randy Alcorn's one-stop handbook for you, your family, and your church.

## THE GRACE AND TRUTH PARADOX
Responding with Christlike Balance
**RANDY ALCORN** ISBN 1-59052-065-3

Living like Christ is a lot to ask! Discover Randy Alcorn's two-point checklist for Christlikeness—and begin to measure everything by the simple test of grace and truth.

## THE TREASURE PRINCIPLE
Discovering the Secret of Joyful Giving
**RANDY ALCORN** ISBN 1-57673-780-2

Bestselling author Randy Alcorn uncovers a revolutionary key to spiritual transformation: joyful giving!
**THE TREASURE PRINCIPLE BIBLE STUDY**
ISBN 1-59052-187-0

## WHAT THE SPIRIT IS SAYING TO THE CHURCHES
**HENRY BLACKABY** ISBN 1-59052-036-X

Learn how to listen to what the Holy Spirit is saying to you and to your church. Don't miss this release from Henry Blackaby, bestselling author of *Experiencing God*.
**WHAT THE SPIRIT IS SAYING TO THE CHURCHES BIBLE STUDY**
ISBN 1-59052-216-8

# BIG CHANGE

Cover Not Final

## How Good Is Good Enough?
**ANDY STANLEY**  ISBN 1-59052-274-5
(Available October 2003)

Find out why Jesus taught that goodness is not even a requirement to enter heaven—and why Christianity is beyond fair.

## A Little Pot of Oil
**JILL BRISCOE**  ISBN 1-59052-234-6
(Available October 2003)

What if He's asking you to pour out more than you can give? Step into the forward motion of God's love—and find the power of the Holy Spirit!

## In the Secret Place
For God and You Alone
**J. OTIS LEDBETTER**  ISBN 1-59052-252-4
(Available September 2003)

Receive answers to some of life's most perplexing questions—and find deeper fellowship alone in the place where God dwells.

## The Air I Breathe
Worship as a Way of Life
**LOUIE GIGLIO**  ISBN 1-59052-153-6

When we are awakened to the wonder of God's character and the cross of Christ, all of life becomes worship unto God.

### OUR JEALOUS GOD
Love That Won't Let Me Go
**BILL GOTHARD** ISBN 1-59052-225-7
(Available October 2003)

God's intense jealousy for you is your highest honor, an
overflowing of sheer grace. And when you understand it better,
it becomes a pathway to countless blessings.

### THE POWER OF CRYING OUT
When Prayer Becomes Mighty
**BILL GOTHARD** ISBN 1-59052-037-8

Bill Gothard explains how a crisis that is humanly impossible
is an opportunity for God to show His power—the moment
you cry out to Him.

### THE FIRE THAT IGNITES
Living in the Power of the Holy Spirit
**TONY EVANS** ISBN 1-59052-083-1

Tony Evans reveals how the Holy Spirit can ignite a fire in
your life today, transforming you from a sleepwalker into
a wide-awake witness for Him!

### GOD IS UP TO SOMETHING GREAT
Turning Your Yesterdays into Better Tomorrows
**TONY EVANS** ISBN 1-59052-038-6

Are you living with regrets? Discover the positives of your past.
Tony Evans shows how God intends to use your experiences—
good, bad, and ugly—to lead you toward His purpose for your life.

SMALL BOOKS
BIG CHANGE

# BIG CHANGE

SMALL BOOKS
BIG CHANGE